A
Literature Un
for

The Cricket
in
Times Square

by George Selden

Written by Susan Onion

Illustrated by Keith Vasconcelles

Teacher Created Materials, Inc.
P.O. Box 1040
Huntington Beach, CA 92647
©1992 *Teacher Created Materials, Inc.*
Made in U.S.A.

ISBN 1-55734-419-1

Table of Contents

Introduction

A good book can touch our lives like a good friend. Within its pages are words and characters that can inspire us to achieve our highest ideals. We can turn to it for companionship, recreation, comfort, and guidance. It can also give us a cherished story to hold in our hearts forever.

In *Literature Units*, great care has been taken to select books that are sure to become good friends!

Teachers who use this unit will find the following features to supplement their own valuable ideas.

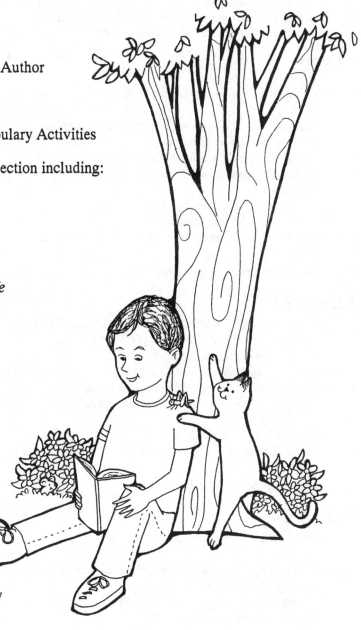

- Sample Lesson Plans

- Pre-Reading Activities

- Biographical Sketch and Picture of the Author

- Book Summary

- Vocabulary Lists and Suggested Vocabulary Activities

- Chapters grouped for study with each section including:
    - *quizzes*
    - *hands-on projects*
    - *cooperative learning activities*
    - *cross-curriculum connections*
    - *extensions into the reader's own life*

- Post-Reading Activities

- Book Report Ideas

- Research Ideas

- Culminating Activity

- Three Different Options for Unit Tests

- Bibliography

- Answer Key

We are confident this unit will be a valuable addition to your planning, and we hope your students will increase the circle of "friends" they have in books!

Sample Lesson Plan

This book divides the chapters in *The Cricket in Times Square* into five sections. Each section has five activities and an accompanying vocabulary list. Below is a sample lesson sequence. Each lesson suggested below can take from one to several days to complete.

LESSON 1

- Introduce and discuss some or all of the pre-reading activities found on page 5.
- Read "About the Author" with your students. (page 6)
- Explain the extension ideas on page 37. These can be used throughout the unit where appropriate.

LESSON 2

- Introduce the vocabulary list for Section 1. (page 8)
- Read chapters 1-3. As you read, place the vocabulary words in the context of the story.
- Choose a vocabulary activity. (page 9)
- Discuss newspapers and do the newspaper search. (page 11)
- Write an adventure story in a team. (page 12)
- Learn about crickets. (page 13)
- Discuss how your students help out their families. (page 14)
- Administer Section 1 quiz. (page 10)

LESSON 3

- Introduce the vocabulary list for Section 2. (page 8)
- Read chapters 4-6. As you read, place the vocabulary words in the context of the story.
- Choose a vocabulary activity. (page 9)
- Write fortunes and bake fortune cookies. (page 16)
- Work as a group to tell stories and learn about storytelling. (page 17)
- Design a cricket cage. (page 18)
- Discuss Chester's view of your town. (page 19)
- Administer Section 2 quiz. (page 15)

LESSON 4

- Introduce the vocabulary list for Section 3. (page 8)
- Read chapters 7-9. As you read, place the vocabulary words in the context of the story.
- Choose a vocabulary activity. (page 9)
- Prepare a Chinese meal. (page 21)
- Discuss the term "fiction." Play the fiction game. (page 22)
- Discuss the book in terms of math. (page 23)
- Role play helping situations. (page 24)
- Administer Section 3 quiz. (page 20)

LESSON 5

- Introduce the vocabulary list for Section 4. (page 8)
- Read chapters 10-12. As you read, place the vocabulary words in the context of the story.
- Choose a vocabulary activity. (page 9)
- Learn about and make a stringed instrument. (page 26)
- Create an ad campaign. (page 27)
- Discuss the book in terms of music. (page 28)
- Discuss fire safety. (page 29)
- Administer Section 4 quiz. (page 25)

LESSON 6

- Introduce vocabulary list for Section 5. (page 8)
- Read chapters 13-15. As you read, place the vocabulary words in the context of the story.
- Choose a vocabulary activity. (page 9)
- Test your sense of smell. (page 31)
- Interview a famous person. (page 32)
- Study a subway map. (page 33)
- Analyze your radio station programming. (page 34)
- Administer Section 5 quiz. (page 30)

LESSON 7

- Assign book and/or research reports. (pages 35 and 36)
- Begin work on culminating activity. (pages 38, 39, 40, 41)

LESSON 8

- Review the book using the activity in Unit Test Option 3. (page 44)
- Administer Unit Tests 1, and/or 2. (pages 42, 43)
- Discuss the test answers.
- Discuss your students' enjoyment of the book.
- Provide a list of related reading for your students. (page 45)

Before the Book

Before you begin reading *The Cricket in Times Square* with your students, do some pre-reading activities to stimulate interest and enhance reading comprehension. Here are some activities that might work well in your class.

1. Predict what the story might be about by hearing the title and looking at the cover.

2. Ask your students if any of them have read other novels written by George Selden.

3. Have students predict whether they think this story is fiction or nonfiction.

4. Talk about what kind of animals might live in a city environment. What types of animals do you think generally inhabit rural areas? Are there some animals that seem to adapt to both areas?

5. Discuss and answer these questions:

   Are you interested in:

   - stories about animals that talk?
   - stories about animals helping humans?
   - stories where characters explore and adapt to new environments?
   - stories about pets?

   Would you ever:

   - work in a newsstand to help your family make money?
   - want a cricket as a pet?
   - write a letter to the New York *Times*?
   - visit Chinatown in New York City by yourself?
   - consider learning to play the violin?

   Have you ever heard a cricket chirping? Where? When? Describe the sound.

6. Locate New York City and Connecticut on a map. What do your students know about New York City? About Connecticut? About Times Square? To better understand the story and visualize the setting, have students research facts about Connecticut and New York: climate, topography, recreation, lifestyles, etc. Research information, maps, and pictures can be displayed on a wall chart or bulletin board. Use the display for reference while reading *The Cricket in Times Square*.

About the Author

George Selden Thompson was born in Hartford, Connecticut on May 14, 1929. He attended the Loomis School from 1943-1947. In 1951, he graduated with a Bachelor of Arts degree from Yale University. Following his graduation from Yale, he traveled to Italy as a Fulbright Scholar and spent the year traveling in Europe. He returned to New York City to begin a career as a writer.

George Selden Thompson adopted the pseudonym George Selden when he started writing, since another writer had already assumed the name of George Thompson. Writing under a different name prevented any confusion between the two writers.

His first printed story was *The Dog That Could Swim Underwater*. This story did not become well-known. Later, at a party, he was encouraged by Noel Coward to "press on." He did, and his next book, *The Cricket in Times Square,* became a great success.

When asked about his writing, George Selden recalls an experience from his childhood. He remembers reading about a subject in one of his school textbooks. He was so interested in the subject that he felt compelled to write a story. Since then, he has often felt driven to his desk to write.

His interests range from archaeology and anthropology to music. It is easy to see how these areas of interest played a part in the plot development of *The Cricket in Times Square*.

George Selden was a recipient of the Christopher Award in 1970 for *Tucker's Countryside*. *The Cricket in Times Square* was named a Newbery Honor Book in 1961.

The Cricket in Times Square

by George Selden
(Dell, 1988)
(Available from Doubleday Dell Seal, Canada; Penguin Books, UK; Transworld Publishers, Australia)

Chester Cricket unexpectedly arrives in the New York City Times Square subway station via a picnic basket from Connecticut. Soon after his arrival he meets and becomes fast friends with Tucker Mouse and Harry Cat, two residents of the subway station. Chester also becomes a pet for Mario Bellini, a boy whose family runs a newsstand in the subway station. Unfortunately, the Bellinis' business is not very successful.

Following Chester's arrival, some new developments take place for the Bellini family. Mario goes on an adventure to Chinatown in search of a new cricket cage for Chester. There he meets an ancient Chinese gentleman who teaches him about Chinese foods and customs. The next morning, Chester is found guilty of eating half of a two-dollar bill from the Bellinis' cash register. A few nights later, there is an unexplained fire in the newsstand after the Bellinis have gone home for the evening. Mama Bellini calls Chester a jinx and blames him for the family's recent bad luck. Chester feels responsible for the Bellinis' misfortune, and wonders what he can do to improve the family's situation.

Tucker suggests that Chester Cricket apply his hidden musical talent. Chester learns to play familiar popular music and performs daily concerts at the newsstand. Mama Bellini forgives Chester after she hears his splendid playing. The people are amazed by Chester's talent, and flock to the Bellini's newsstand. The Bellinis are able to sell many newspapers and magazines as they attract new customers.

After a week of concerts, Chester begins to feel homesick for the meadows of Connecticut. He plans his last recital for Mario, says farewell to Harry and Tucker, and boards a train to Connecticut with plans of a reunion with his city friends someday in the countryside.

Vocabulary Lists

On this page are vocabulary lists which correspond to each sectional grouping of chapters. Vocabulary activity ideas can be found on page 9 of this book.

SECTION 1
Chapters 1-3

anxiously	peculiar
concluded	plucked
eavesdropping	rummaged
forlornly	scornfully
furiously	scrounging
glimmering	subsided
liverwurst	subway
niche	wistfully

SECTION 2
Chapters 4-6

abrupt	knickknacks
acquaintance	leery
amidst	urging
ashamed	looming
avalanche	lurched
clustered	novelties
craned	pagoda
genius	spire
kimonos	venturing

SECTION 3
Chapters 7-9

accuse	loot
chopsticks	luscious
compartments	mulberry
contentment	rap
disbelief	skinflint
keen	solemn
evidence	soufflé
galoshes	sternly
glided	rumply

SECTION 4
Chapters 10-12

amateur	glumly
blurted	implore
buffet	indignantly
castanets	jinx
"chamber music"	limbered
climax	luminous
commuters	meekly
composition	precious
darted	recital
dumbfounded	rhythm
dwindled	rodent
frayed	strains
sublime	salvage

SECTION 5
Chapters 13-15

celebrity	midget
dazed	recital
encore	retiring
entomologist	scornfully
fascinated	smidgin
fidgeted	stock
intermission	throngs

Vocabulary Activity Ideas

You can help your students learn and retain the vocabulary in *The Cricket in Times Square* by providing them with interesting vocabulary activities. Here are a few ideas to try.

❑ **True or False Definitions**—This game should be played before students have looked up or become familiar with a new list of words. The goal of this game is to guess which student is presenting the correct definition. Make up three definition cards for each vocabulary word. One of these cards should have the correct definition. Be sure to mark this card as special. Select three students to be on the definition presentation panel and hand each student on the panel a definition card. Write the new vocabulary word on the board for the class to see. The students on the panel take turns reading their definition cards to the class. The student with the true definition must read the card as written. The students who hold the unmarked, incorrect definition cards may make up another fictional definition if they choose. The remaining students in the class then vote to see which is the true definition. Points may be earned by correct guesses. Rotate students so each student has a chance to be on the panel.

❑ **Group Short Stories**—Divide your class into groups. Ask the groups to create short stories which include all of the vocabulary words assigned. See which team can make up the shortest, funniest, or most exciting story.

❑ **Vocabulary Bingo**—Hand out blank bingo grids to students. Have them place one vocabulary word in each space on the grid. Students may place the words in any order on the sheet. Then randomly choose and read the vocabulary definitions. A student wins by covering a row or column of words as the definitions are read.

❑ **Pictionary**—Students take turns drawing pictures that illustrate the vocabulary words while the rest of the class tries to guess which word is being illustrated.

❑ **One Sentence Challenge**—Challenge your students to create one sentence using as many vocabulary words as possible. Be sure that the sentences make sense!

❑ **Vocabulary Charades**—Have students act out vocabulary words while the rest of the class attempts to guess which words are being portrayed.

❑ **Team Presentations**—Divide the class into teams and assign each team groups of words to present to the rest of the class. Teams are responsible for looking up the assigned words and designing a presentation which will help everyone remember the meanings. Teams may use drama, drawings, songs, rhymes, or any other creative approach in their presentations.

❑ **Puzzles and Word Searches**—Have students create crossword puzzles or word searches using vocabulary from their word lists. This may be done individually or in small groups. Have students exchange puzzles and word searches and solve. (Provide answer keys.)

❑ **Vocabulary Bee!**—Challenge your students to a **Vocabulary Bee**, played using spelling bee rules, but with players defining the vocabulary words as well.

You probably have many more ideas to add to this list. Try them! See if experiencing vocabulary on a personal level increases your students' vocabulary interest and retention!

Quiz Time

1. On the back of this page, write a one paragraph summary of the major events in each chapter of this section. Then complete the rest of the questions on this page.

2. How does Mario help his family?

    _____

    _____

3. There are five items kept in the Bellinis' newsstand. List three of these items and explain the Bellinis' reasons for keeping them.

    _____

    _____

4. Do you think that Paul knew that he gave Mario too much money for the Sunday *Times*? If so, why didn't Paul wait for his change?

    _____

    _____

5. Write a brief characterization of Tucker Mouse.

    _____

    _____

6. How does Mario discover Chester Cricket?

    _____

    _____

7. How does Mama Bellini feel about Mario's new pet?

    _____

    _____

8. What foods does Chester eat that are unlikely meals for a cricket?

    _____

    _____

9. If you were Mario, would you want to have a cricket as a pet? Explain your answer.

    _____

    _____

10. On the back of this paper, explain how Chester came to be in New York City.

Newspaper Search

The Bellinis' newsstand sold newspapers and magazines which provided a source of important information to the people commuting through the Times Square subway station. To learn more about the different parts of the newspaper and where to look for information, you will work with your team to find the items listed below. Each team will be supplied with one complete newspaper. When you locate an item in the newspaper, list the page and section on the line. Happy hunting!

_____ a map

_____ the name of your state

_____ a girl's name

_____ a picture of a dog

_____ a puzzle

_____ an important job

_____ a picture of a famous person

_____ the name of another country

_____ something to drink

_____ a capital letter "M"

_____ a price over $39.00

_____ the word Thursday

_____ a sentence with 2 nouns

_____ the name of a movie

_____ a food that is sweet

_____ a sport's score

_____ someone helping another person or animal

_____ a phone number

_____ a picture of something funny

_____ a word in bold print

Trapped!

When Chester Cricket first meets Tucker Mouse, he tells his story of being trapped in a picnic basket and of traveling to New York City on the train.

Imagine that you are trapped in a picnic basket and are about to experience quite an adventure.

- Where does your adventure begin?

- What kind of goodies are in the basket?

- Where does your journey take you?

- What kind of creature are you?

- Are you discovered or do you make a narrow escape?

- Where does your adventure end?

In teams, work together to write an adventure story. Brainstorm and outline your ideas to include everyone's input before writing. Each team will need a reader to read the questions listed above, a secretary to record the story as the team dictates, a checker to be sure that the questions are all answered, and a monitor to be sure that each team member has ideas included in the story.

When your story is written, practice reading it so that every member of your team will have a part when you share your story with the rest of the class!

The Common Cricket

Crickets are found in nearly every part of the world where plants grow. The most common cricket in North and South America is the field cricket.

The common cricket has six legs and its body is divided into three parts. The first section is the head, which holds the antennae (or feelers) and the compound eyes. The cricket's mouth is made up of a complex system of jaws used to perform the functions needed for eating. The middle section is the thorax. This is where the three pairs of legs and the two sets of wings are joined. The rear section is the abdomen. The abdomen contains the organs for digestion, breathing, and mating. The eardrums are found near the knee on the front pair of legs. The eardrums help the cricket tell the distance and direction of other singing crickets.

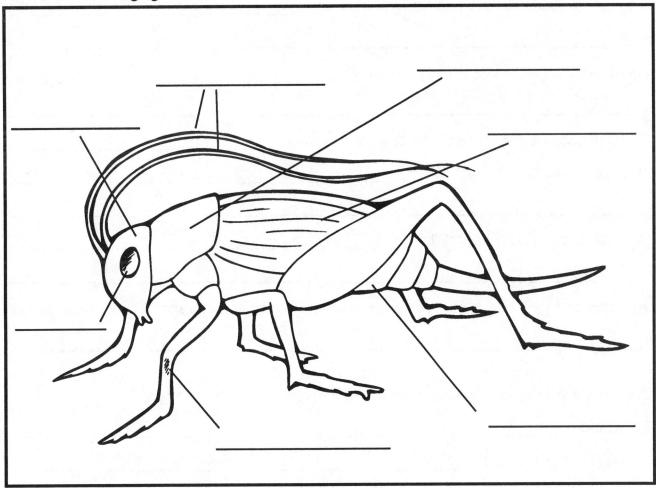

Label your cricket using the information given in the paragraph above. Use the body parts listed to complete your diagram.

abdomen	**antennae**	**compound eye**
eardrum	**head**	**thorax**
wing		

Create your own cricket using pipe cleaners, craft foam balls, and other materials that will make it look as realistic as possible.

Helping Out

> Mario helped his family by working in his father's newsstand every Saturday night. By keeping the newsstand open later into the evening, Papa hoped to attract more business.
>
> Many of us have jobs that also help our families. Some of us help by setting the table for dinner or by washing the dishes. Sharing these chores with family members makes everyone's work a little easier. Think about your chores at home and answer the questions listed below.

What jobs or chores do you have to do in your house? _____

_____

How is doing these chores a help to your family? _____

_____

Would the jobs get done if you did not do them? By whom? _____

What job do you like the most? Why? _____

_____

What job do you like the least? Why? _____

_____

Are there some jobs that you work on together with your parents or sisters and brothers? What are they?

_____

If you could make up the job assignments in your house, which jobs would you give:

   yourself? _____

   your brothers or sisters? _____

   your parents? _____

   your pet? _____

Do you think it is important that people are assigned chores in order to help out in a household? Why or why not?

_____

_____

Quiz Time

1. On the back of this page, write a one paragraph summary of the major events in each chapter of this section. Then complete the rest of the questions on this page.

2. Why does the friendship between Tucker and Harry surprise Chester?

   _____

   _____

3. Harry Cat says he is concerned about the future of the Bellinis' newsstand. Why does he have this concern?

   _____

   _____

4. How does Chester feel after his first view of Times Square?

   _____

   _____

5. What was Chester's usual diet in the meadow?

   _____

   _____

6. Why is Mr. Smedley impressed with Chester Cricket?

   _____

   _____

7. Why does Mario look for a cricket cage in Chinatown?

   _____

   _____

8. Mario assumes that the beautiful cricket cage would be very expensive, yet Sai Fong sells it to Mario for only 15 cents. Why do you think Sai Fong is so generous?

   _____

   _____

9. List four words that describe Sai Fong.

   _____   _____

   _____   _____

10. Do you think Sai Fong's story about the wise man who became a cricket is true? On the back of this paper, explain why or why not.

Good Fortune

"Good Luck is coming your way. Be ready."

chapter 11

Mario received this fortune in a cookie the first time he visited Sai Fong. Within a few days, Chester Cricket and the Bellinis' newsstand achieved fame and fortune.

Have you ever received a fortune that seems to come true? Do you believe in the art of fortune telling?

In this activity, you will be making your own fortune cookies. First, you will need to make up fortunes and write them on small slips of paper. Then you will need to follow the recipe below to make the cookies. Be creative in your fortune telling. Good luck may come your way, too.

Fortune Cookie Recipe

Preheat oven to 350^0 F (180^0 C).

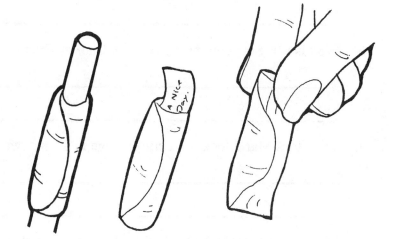

Mix together until creamy:

$^1/_4$ cup (60 mL) butter

$^1/_2$ cup (125 mL) confectioners' sugar

Add:

3 egg whites (unbeaten)

$^1/_2$ cup (125 mL) flour

1 teaspoon (5 mL) vanilla or almond extract

Beat until smooth. Drop dough by tablespoons onto greased cookie sheet. Be sure to leave a lot of space between cookies. Bake for 8-10 minutes or until edges turn golden brown. Remove from oven and turn cookies out onto a flat surface to be shaped. Shape cookies by rolling them around the end of a clean wooden spoon handle. Cookies must be shaped while they are still warm, so work quickly. (You may need to hold the cookies in the curled position around the spoon handle for a few seconds to ensure that they will maintain their shapes.) After you remove the spoon handle, insert the fortune strip and pinch the ends of the cookie.

Makes about 1 dozen cookies.

Storytelling

When Mario visited Sai Fong in Chinatown, Sai Fong told Mario a story explaining how the cricket came to be. Mario and Chester both enjoyed this explanation. Storytelling can be an interesting and fun way to learn about past events, share thoughts about the future, or to explain the unknown.

For this activity, you will be working in groups of five to make up a story explaining how something was created or came into existence. Each group will be assigned a tape recorder and stopwatch while telling the story. The stories will be recorded so that they can be played back later for the entire class.

Once the teams are arranged, each team member should draw from a box a number from one to five. The student who draws the number one will begin telling the story. He/she will have three minutes to start. At the end of the three minutes, the student with the number two will pick up where the first storyteller left off and continue telling the story. Continue the sequence until each member of the team has had a turn. The student who drew the number five must complete the story. Team members should take turns running the stopwatch and tape recorder. It is important to be quiet while the storyteller is speaking so you can produce a clear recording to play for the class. It may be helpful to stop the tape recorder between each person's turn, so the new storyteller can prepare an idea before continuing the story.

Teams may choose one of the following story ideas or create one of their own.

1.   How did the pig get its nose?

2.   Why does the skunk have a stripe?

3.   Why does the cat purr?

4.   How did the giraffe get its long neck?

5.   How did the spider learn to spin a web?

6.   Why does the firefly light up at night?

7.   How did the raccoon get two black eyes?

8.   How did the owl become so wise?

If you enjoy telling these short stories about animals, you may enjoy reading *Aesop's Fables*. Ask your librarian or teacher for more information. Once you are familiar with the way a fable is written, you may want to create a group book of fables. Be sure to give it a unique title. Each member of the group can contribute two or three fables, complete with illustrations.

A Classy Cage

When Sai Fong brought out the cricket cage, Mario knew that it would be perfect for Chester. He wanted it so much that he tingled all over. Sai Fong explained that it was an ancient cage which once belonged to the Emperor of China. The cage was shaped like a small pagoda with seven tiers. It was painted red and green with a golden spire. There was a small gate with a latch at one side.

What do you think a cricket cage should be shaped like? A bird house? An apartment building? A spool of thread? What colors would you paint your cricket cage? How big would it be?

Use the space below to design your own version of the perfect cricket cage. As you sketch your design, think about what materials and colors you will need to make your cage. After you are finished, use your sketch and plans to construct an actual cage.

Your Town

In Chapter 4, Tucker and Harry take Chester Cricket to visit New York City's Times Square. This was Chester's first view of a thriving, crowded city. He was overwhelmed by the lights, sounds, and motions. He closed his eyes and thought of his peaceful home in the country. Chester also had difficulty riding on the subway train with Mario on the way to Chinatown. He was unfamiliar with the lurching of the train and fell from Mario's pocket. Although Chester was a country cricket who was unaccustomed to the city crowds and sounds, he was curious and interested in seeing what the city had to offer.

Imagine that Chester has arrived in a picnic basket on your doorstep, and that you are the personal guide who will take him on a tour of your home town. Think about the following questions. Write a plan showing how you would conduct the tour, where you would go, and what you would see. Then, try the activity at the bottom of this page.

- How would you travel with Chester around your town so that he would feel comfortable?

- What special places in your town would you want to show Chester?

- To whom would you want to introduce Chester? Why?

- What would Chester find most surprising about your town?

- Where would you take Chester for lunch? Why?

- If you took Chester to visit your school, what would he like most about it?

- Do you think Chester would feel at home in your town?

- What would your friends and family think about Chester?

- Do you think Chester would want to come back to visit your town? Why or why not?

- If Chester decided to stay with you, what permanent arrangements would you make for him?

Activity: Make a travel brochure about your town that would be sure to interest others enough to want to visit the sites. The Chamber of Commerce and local travel agencies may provide you with pamphlets and brochures in which you can find helpful information for preparing your own brochure.

Quiz Time

1. On the back of this paper, write a one paragraph summary of the major events in each chapter of this section. Then complete the rest of the questions on this page.

2. How does Tucker feel about Chester's new cage?

    _____

    _____

3. What does Chester find for Tucker to use as a pillow?

    _____

4. At the end of chapter seven, Chester says that he is beginning to enjoy New York. Why do you suppose this is so?

    _____

    _____

5. Chester has to make some choices after eating the two dollar bill from the cash register. List two of the ideas that Tucker suggests.

    _____

    _____

6. Do you think it was a fair decision to make Mario replace the money that Chester ruined? Why or why not?

    _____

    _____

7. Explain Sai Fong's solution to Mario's problem with Chester.

    _____

8. What attitude about money do Tucker Mouse and Mama Bellini share?

    _____

9. Why does Mario decide to return to Chinatown to visit Sai Fong?

    _____

10. How was Mario's dinner with Sai Fong different from the dinner he might have had with his family? List three differences.

    _____

    _____

    _____

Chinese Dinner

In Chapter 9 of *The Cricket in Times Square*, Mario visits Sai Fong in Chinatown. When he arrives, Sai Fong and an old Chinese gentleman are preparing dinner. They invite Mario to join them in their traditional feast. Mario is given a robe to wear, eats with chopsticks, and tries many traditional Chinese foods.

Ask your students if any of them have eaten in a Chinese restaurant. Ask them what it was like, what foods they ate, and how the menu differed from that of other restaurants.

Tell your students that they will be preparing a Chinese meal in class. You can have your class work together to choose Chinese recipes and to make a list of items which will be needed to prepare them, or, you may use the foods, utensils, and the simple recipe listed below to prepare your meal.

You will need a wok, a hot plate, and a toaster oven, or have access to a kitchen to prepare these foods.

Foods

*box of rice	Chicken with Chinese Vegetables *(recipe below)*
*frozen egg rolls	tea
*Prepare as directed.	fortune cookies

Utensils

chopsticks	paper or foam bowls
wooden spoons	cookie sheet
pot	pot holders
plates	tea kettle
measuring cups and spoons	

Chicken with Chinese Vegetables

(Sample servings for 10 students)

1 pound (500 g) chicken (diced)
2 tablespoons (20 mL) soy sauce
3 tablespoons (45 mL) vegetable oil
(2) 10 ounce (300 g) boxes frozen Chinese or Oriental stir fry vegetables
6 ounce (180 g) bag almonds

Put oil in wok over medium-high heat. When oil is hot, add chicken and saute until lightly browned. Remove chicken.

Place vegetables in wok. Stir until lightly cooked. Add chicken and almonds. Sprinkle with soy sauce. Continue stirring until heated through.

Serve over rice in small bowls.

Enjoy your Chinese feast using some traditional Chinese customs. Students should research and report to the class information they find about how meals are prepared, traditional utensils, and Chinese etiquette. Try to adopt some of these traditions during your class dinner.

Fiction Fun

The Cricket in Times Square is a fictional story. The term "fiction" means that the story is made up and that it did not actually take place. There are many clues in *The Cricket in Times Square* that lead us to believe that the story is fictional. An obvious clue is that we know that animals do not speak, yet the animal characters in the story talk to one another.

For this game you will be working in teams. Each team will be given 10 minutes to find examples from the story which prove that this is a fiction book. Make a list of your team's ideas.

When the 10 minutes are up, each team will present one of the examples from the team list. Examples may not be repeated. After each team has presented an idea, return to the first team to present its second example. Continue taking turns until the last idea is presented. The team that has the most original examples wins.

Game Rules

1. Teams may not add ideas to their list after the 10 minutes are up and the sharing has begun.

2. If an idea is repeated, the team has 10 seconds to present another example from its list or the team misses its turn.

3. If an example does not make sense, the rest of the class can vote to decide if the team must present a new idea.

4. Team members within teams must take turns presenting their examples to the class.

5. Teams earn one point for each original idea that they present to the class.

Tucker's Life Savings

Tucker Mouse collected a small fortune while living in the Times Square subway station. Through his scrounging, he was able to collect two half dollars, five quarters, two dimes, six nickels and eighteen pennies. Tucker's life savings amounted to a grand total of $2.93.

What other combinations of coins could Tucker have scrounged to equal $2.93? What is the fewest number of coins Tucker could have collected? What is the greatest number?

Complete the chart below by reading down each column and finding the number of coins that are missing. Remember that your total for each column must equal $2.93.

number of coins scrounged	15 coins	20 coins	44 coins	fewest possible coins	greatest number of possible coins
fifty cent pieces	3	0			
quarters		8	4		
dimes	3				
nickels	2	0			
pennies			28		

Which combination of coins do you think Tucker would prefer to have in his drain pipe? Explain your choice.

Helping a Friend

After Chester Cricket accidentally ate a two dollar bill from the Bellinis' cash register, Tucker attempted to help his friend brainstorm a solution to his problem. Tucker's suggestions to steal money from the lunch counter to replace the two dollars or to blame the missing money on a thief, did not satisfy Chester.

The friends continued to work on the problem together. When Harry suggested that Tucker should donate his scrounging money, Tucker was hesitant, but he agreed to help his friend.

Can you think of a time when you helped a friend solve a problem? What did you do to help? Did your friend feel better after your help? Was the problem solved?

Role play the following situations in your class. Pretend that your friend has come to you asking for your help to solve the problem. After you have tried these situations, write down how you solved them. Then make up some of your own scenarios to role play. Share these with the class.

Situation	How We Solved It
Your friend has to stay after school for shooting spitballs and doesn't know how to tell his/her parents.	
Your friend wants to play basketball after school, but she has to walk to the babysitters to pick up her little brother.	
While playing baseball, your friend accidentally broke a neighbor's window.	
Your friend refuses to allow a new student to join a popular club. Now your friend feels badly that he/she hurt the new student's feelings.	
Your friend cheated on a spelling test in class and feels guilty.	

Quiz Time

1. On the back of this paper, write a one paragraph summary of the major events in each chapter of this section. Then complete the rest of the questions on this page.

2. List at least four of the foods that Tucker Mouse scrounged for the dinner party.

   _____

   _____

3. Why are iced soft drinks such a treat for Chester, Tucker, and Harry?

   _____

   _____

4. How does Tucker learn to play familiar songs?

   _____

   _____

5. Who puts out the fire at the Bellinis' newsstand?

   _____

   _____

6. Why does Mama Bellini call Chester a jinx?

   _____

   _____

7. Why does Chester feel guilty about the fire?

   _____

   _____

8. What makes Mama Bellini change her mind about making Chester leave?

   _____

   _____

9. Describe Mr. Smedley's reaction upon hearing Chester "sing."

   _____

   _____

10. How would you react if you heard a cricket playing a familiar song at a newsstand in your town? Why would you react this way?

    _____

    _____

The Sweet Sound of Music

The cricket is one of many insects which is able to produce a musical sound. The cricket produces its musical chirp by opening and closing its wings. The wings rub together, causing small, comb-like ridges to make the chirping sound that we hear when we listen to a cricket. This small creature is able to change its song by rubbing together either some or all of the ridges on its wings.

A stringed instrument produces sound in a similar manner. When a string on a guitar is plucked, it causes the string to vibrate. These vibrations are sent into the air and are interpreted as musical sound. The pitch (how high or low the note sounds) depends upon how rapidly or slowly the string is vibrating. A guitar player can change a string's pitch by holding a string tightly to the neck of the guitar. This shortens the string's vibrating length, making the string vibrate faster. A string that vibrates faster produces a higher pitch. Another way to change pitch is to alter the string's thickness.

To demonstrate how pitch is changed in stringed instruments, try the following experiments.

Experiment A

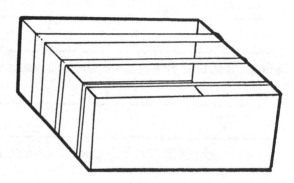

Materials: three rubber bands of equal length but different thicknesses; a cigar box with the top removed; craft knife

Procedure: Cut three equidistant grooves on each of the two shorter top edges of the box. Place each rubber band lengthwise in the grooves and around the box, as shown. Pluck each rubber band and note the sound. Explain the differences.

Experiment B

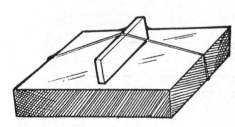

Materials: a 10" (25 cm) length of plywood or strong cardboard; a piece of cardboard at least 3" (8 cm) in length; 1 yd. (1 m) string

Procedure: Tie the string tightly around the length of the board. Place the cardboard strip upright between the string and the board, as shown in the picture. How many different sounds can you make with your instrument? How can you change the note's pitch (make the note higher or lower)? What happens when you remove the piece of cardboard? What happens when you tighten or loosen the string?

Try using dental floss, elastic, rope, or other string-like materials in place of the string to see if you achieve the same results.

Experiment C

Sound is produced by a vibrating object. It travels in waves in all directions, and can travel through solids, liquids, and gases. Test some of these ideas and present your findings to the class. For example, strike a tuning fork against the palm of your hand. Place it to your ear. Through what medium must it travel in order for the sound to reach your ear? Strike the tuning fork and touch it to a desk. Do you hear any sound? Describe it. Now, strike the tuning fork and lower it into a pan of water. What happens?

Research how sound is produced in woodwind, brass, and percussion instruments. If possible, make a model of one of these types of instruments and show the class how the sound is produced.

Advertising

The letter Mr. Smedley wrote to the New York *Times* brought sudden fame to Chester Cricket and the Bellini family. Although it was only a letter written to the newspaper's music editor, the result was free advertising for Chester's concerts. Without advertising, many people who attended the concerts would not have been aware of Chester's amazing talent.

If you were to become an advertising agent for Chester Cricket, how would you interest people to see Chester's performance? What technique would you use to "sell" Chester to the public? What advertising method might you use to reach the most people?

Would you:

- Write a newspaper advertisement?

- Design and distribute posters?

- Make a radio commercial?

- Make a public speech?

- Write and produce a television advertisement?

- Design a magazine advertising campaign?

- Design and put up billboards?

Work in teams of two to plan an advertising campaign for Chester Cricket. Decide which method or methods of advertising you would use; then design a presentation for the class.

COME TO SEE THE

AMAZING
MUSICAL CRICKET

Concerts: Daily 8:00 AM and 4:30 PM

TIMES SQUARE SUBWAY STATION

Bellini's Newsstand

In Concert

Chester worked with Tucker to decide which songs he would play for his concerts in the newsstand. He learned new music by listening to the radio. This gave him a broad base of popular music from which to draw ideas.

If you were to help Chester plan his concert today, what kind of music would you have him play? Remember that you want Chester's concerts to appeal to the broad range of listeners who might be passing through the Times Square subway station.

Work in teams to outline a concert program for Chester. Choose five songs to include in your concert. Think about your reasons for choosing each song and about the audience your songs might appeal to. Fill in the chart below.

Song Title	Artist/Musician	Who would this appeal to?	Why did you choose this song?

When you have made your musical selections, you might want to make a demo tape of what Chester would play.

How might your song choices change if Chester were holding his concert in your school cafeteria?

_____

_____

List on the back of this paper the song titles you would choose instead.

28

Fire Safety

Papa Bellini kept a box of kitchen matches in the newsstand for lighting his pipe. These matches posed little danger when no one was in the newsstand, but on the night of the dinner party, Chester, Tucker, and Harry were unexpected visitors. While dancing, Tucker accidently bumped into the box, causing the matches to fall to the cement floor. Some of the matches were ignited and set some nearby newspapers on fire. Chester, Tucker, and Harry found themselves trapped by the flames. Fortunately, Chester kept his wits and set off the alarm clock which attracted attention to the newsstand and brought help.

Think about what possible fire hazards exist in your house. Would any of them be more or less hazardous if an unexpected visitor, like Tucker Mouse, were prowling around your house? Explain why.

_____

_____

_____

Do you think Papa Bellini should have left the matches in the newsstand? Explain why or why not.

_____

_____

_____

Do you have emergency numbers posted in your house? Where?

_____

_____

_____

Think About It:

What escape plans do you have in case of a fire in your home? How do you leave your room? Do you have more than one escape route? Where does your family meet? What do you do if you are home alone? Where do you go for help?

On the back of this paper, outline your family's escape plan or draw a floor plan of the escape route you would use in case of fire. If you don't have an escape plan, discuss this with your family and describe a plan you think would work best.

Quiz Time

1. On the back of this paper, write a one paragraph summary of the major events in each chapter of this section. Then complete the rest of the questions on this page.

2. How does Mr. Smedley's letter to the New York *Times* help the Bellini family?

   _____

   _____

3. Why is it important for Chester to play "human" music?

   _____

   _____

4. How does Chester feel about all of the attention he receives while playing for the crowds in the subway station?

   _____

   _____

5. What events occur that make Chester feel homesick for Connecticut?

   _____

   _____

6. How does Harry know that Chester is upset?

   _____

   _____

7. What curious effect does Chester's last concert have on the people passing by the newsstand?

   _____

   _____

8. Describe one of the games that Mario played with Chester.

   _____

   _____

9. How does Mario know that Chester has left?

   _____

   _____

10. Do you think the Bellinis' newsstand will be successful without Chester's concerts? Explain your answer.

   _____

   _____

Smells

When Chester traveled in a picnic basket from Connecticut to New York, he was buried underneath sandwiches and was unable to see where he was going. As Chester stepped onto the train on his way back to Connecticut, Tucker asked him how he would know when he arrived at his home. Chester was not concerned. He said, "I'll smell the trees and I'll feel the air, and I'll know." Chester could depend on his senses to help him recognize a familiar environment.

How well trained are your senses? For this activity you will be testing your sense of smell. You will be working in groups of five. Each group will be given five different samples to smell. After you have smelled a sample, write down your guess as to what the cup contains. Fill in your guesses below.

Sample 1	
Sample 2	
Sample 3	
Sample 4	
Sample 5	

When your chart is complete, compare your answers with those of your teammates. Then open the cups to view the ingredients. Who has the most accurate sense of smell? Which ingredients did you guess incorrectly? Were you surprised by any of the ingredients contained in the cups?

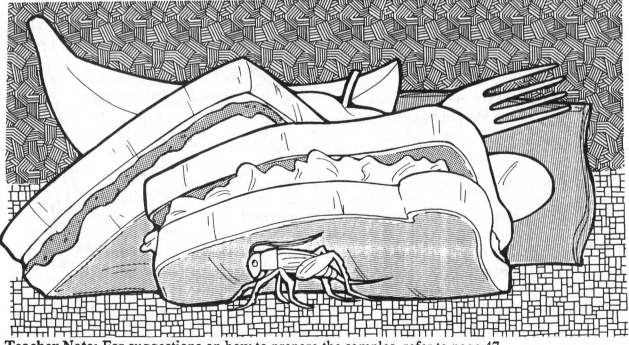

Teacher Note: For suggestions on how to prepare the samples, refer to page 47.

Interviews With the Famous

In Chapter 13 of *The Cricket in Times Square*, the commuters in the Times Square subway station discovered Chester's musical talent. Newspapers, radio stations, and television broadcasts carried stories of Chester's remarkable ability. This publicity attracted many people to come and see the famous cricket. Although Chester enjoyed performing, he was not entirely happy with all of the attention he received from the crowds.

How would you feel about becoming famous like Chester? What would it be like? Would you enjoy the constant attention?

For this activity you will be working in teams of two. Choose a famous person by using library reference books, biographies, or famous people you have learned about in history, science, art, music, literature, etc. One member of the team will be the reporter and one member will be the famous person. This will require some research into the life of the interviewee. Work together to design an interview. Use the questions listed below as a starting point; then add more questions and ideas of your own. Think of a creative way to introduce the famous person and his or her talent. Plan on a closing for your interview. Once you have planned your interview, practice your parts so you will be well prepared when you make your presentation to the class.

- How has becoming famous changed your life?

- Do your friends treat you differently now that you are well known?

- Tell me about the event that helped you to become famous.

- What are some of the difficulties that you have encountered now that you are in the public eye?

- How did you discover and practice your talent?

- Who has supported you most in developing your talent?

- What do you like most about being a celebrity?

- Do you have any special secrets to your success that you would like to share with our audience?

Maps

The New York City subway system is one of the most extensive in the world. There are 237 miles of subway tracks connecting all parts of the city.

Below is a portion of a map of the New York City subway system. You will need colored pencils, crayons, or markers for this activity. Follow the directions given below.

• Trace in red the route Mario might have taken from Times Square to Chinatown.

• Trace in green the route Chester probably took from Times Square to Grand Central Station.

• Find a partner. Choose a route other than one you have already outlined on your map. Without showing your partner your map, give directions from one location to another. Have your partner attempt to draw your directions on his or her map using a pencil. Do not watch what your partner is drawing. After you are finished, compare yours and your partner's maps. Then have your partner try the same exercise.

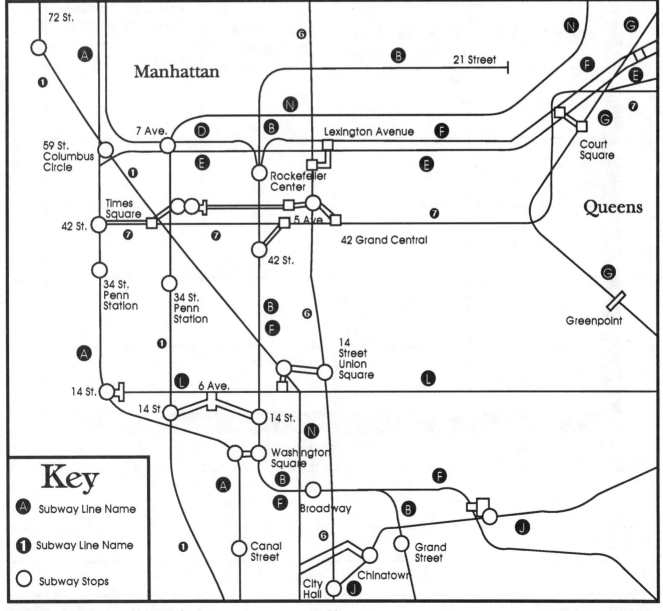

On the Radio

In *The Cricket in Times Square,* the programs on the radio provided a variety of information and entertainment to listeners. Before finding a music station, Tucker Mouse scanned a news report, a quiz show, an amateur hour, and a play. In the evenings, Chester Cricket used the radio as a tool to learn new pieces of music to perform at his concerts. He was able to listen to and learn about many different styles of music due to the wide selection of programming.

How are the programs on the radio in *The Cricket in Times Square* different from the programs commonly broadcast on the radio now? What kind of information is presented now? What different kinds of music can you find?

For this activity you will listen to the radio for one hour and fill in the chart below. You should listen to at least five different stations. Be sure to listen to each station for at least ten minutes.

Station Name	Listening Time (ex. 1:00 - 1:10 pm)	What was playing?	Would you choose to listen to this station? Why or why not?

Compare your listening chart to the kind of programming that Tucker Mouse listened to. Why do you think radio programming might have changed from the time *The Cricket in Times Square* took place to now?

_____

_____

_____

Research Ideas

Describe three things you read in *The Cricket in Times Square* that you would like to learn more about.

1. _____

2. _____

3. _____

George Selden writes about a variety of people, places, and ideas as seen through Chester Cricket's eyes. Further research into these topics will enhance your understanding of the ideas and characters in the story.

Research one or more of the items you named above, or choose one of the ideas listed below. You may work in teams or independently. Be prepared to share the results of your research with your classmates in the form or an oral presentation.

- New York City
- Times Square
- Chinatown
- Connecticut countryside
- New York subway system
- trains
- New York City newspapers
- stringed instruments
- opera
- Grand Central Station
- newspapers

- mulberry trees
- crickets
- fortune cookies
- Orpheus
- superstitions
- "long hairs"
- Chinese foods
- Chinese traditions
- Chinese people
- advertising
- fire safety

Book Report Ideas

There are many ways to do a book report. After you have finished reading *The Cricket in Times Square*, choose one method of reporting that interests you. You may find that although your entire class read the same book, there are many different ideas and opinions about the story to share.

- **Sell it!**

Record a two-minute public service announcement or commercial message to sell the book to the public. Include music or background sound effects in your presentation to make it exciting and attractive to your listeners. Remember that your audience can hear you, but not see you.

- **Pen Pal**

Write a letter to a character in *The Cricket in Times Square*. Tell him/her how different or similar his/her life is compared to yours. Discuss some of the activities or adventures your character has experienced that you might like to try.

- **Puppet Presentation**

Groups of students choose a favorite passage or scene in *The Cricket in Times Square*. The groups then design their own puppets and script to present the scene through a puppet play. The individual scenes can be linked together to form a progression of scenes to present the story to another class.

- **Game Time**

Create a board game using vocabulary, information, and characters from *The Cricket in Times Square*. Display and play the game with classmates.

- **Read All About It**

Write a book review of *The Cricket in Times Square* which could be printed in a newspaper. Include the who, what, when, where, why, and how information from the story, but remember to also make your write-up so interesting that the reader will want to read the story.

- **Become a Character**

This report takes the form of a panel discussion. Each student on the panel adopts the personality of one character in *The Cricket in Times Square*. The remaining students may ask the panel questions about specific scenes in the story or about something totally unrelated, such as what he/she had for breakfast, or what television shows he/she likes to watch.

- **Trace the Path**

Design a map to show where the characters in *The Cricket in Times Square* live and where they travel during the story. Include a key to explain any symbols or pictures.

- **Character Art**

Choose a character to present. Carve from wood, model from clay, or paint a picture of that character. Write a brief character sketch to accompany your art work.

- **On the Wall**

Design a wall mural as a class. Discuss important scenes from *The Cricket in Times Square*. Vote on which scenes should be included to tell the story in the mural. Assign groups to work together to create the individual scenes.

Extra! Extra! Extension Ideas!

The following activities can be integrated into your unit as extensions to the activities already outlined in this book. Some of them may require a little more footwork or planning before presenting to your class. The ideas are in no particular sequence or order.

- Make traditional ice cream sodas (recipe given in chapter 5).

- Share a copy of the New York *Times* with your class. Create your own classroom newspaper modelled after it.

- Look at a Chinese restaurant's menu. Design your own Chinese menus.

- Have a Chinese person come to speak to your class about his/her culture.

- Bring in tapes of old radio show programming to play for your students.

- Plan a scavenger hunt to "scrounge" for objects like Tucker mouse.

- Keep a cricket in the classroom for students to study. Vote on a name for your new class pet.

- Play classical string ensemble and country "fiddle" music for your students. Compare the two styles of music and methods of playing the violin.

- Have a student or musician who plays a stringed instrument speak to and play for your class.

- Read some of George Selden's sequels (*Tucker's Countryside, Chester Cricket's New Home, Chester Cricket's Pigeon Ride*).

- Read *Charlotte's Web* by E.B. White. Compare and contrast Tucker and Templeton mouse.

- Watch the film of *The Cricket in Times Square*. Compare and contrast the novel and the film version.

- Take a field trip to your local newspaper, ride on a train or subway, or attend a classical string concert.

Class Newspaper

The next four pages contain an outline and activities to guide the students in writing, publishing, and distributing their own newspaper. Before beginning this project, have your students study a real newspaper. Discuss the parts, article types, and format. A field trip to your local newspaper facility can also give your students additional information on how a news story makes it from reporter to publication.

Organize: What do we want to write about?

Decide with your class which sections and types of stories will be included in your paper. Some ideas might be:

>   *News Section*—world, national, local
>   *Sports Section*—school or local sports events
>   *Letters to the Editor*
>   *Advertisements*—school bake sales or upcoming
>   school concerts and events
>   *Advise Column*—"Dear..."
>   *Information Section*—school calendar, menu, etc.
>   *Feature Articles*—television, movie, or book reviews;
>   comics; puzzles; interviews

Format: How do we want to write it?

Before you begin writing, your class will also need to make the following decisions:

>   *Name of your newspaper*
>   *Length of the paper*
>   *Length of the sections and stories*
>   *Publication date*

Staffing: Who is going to write it?

Story assignments will need to be made. Help students brainstorm and choose story ideas so your newspaper will have a variety of articles.

>   *Reporters*
>   *Feature writers*
>   *Proofreaders*
>   *Editors*

Note: This outline is used with permission and based on materials by Becky Hayes Boober, Maine Newspaper in Education Programs, Augusta, Maine, 1986.

TCM-137 *Newspaper Reporters* and TCM-138 *Newspapers* (fifteen 11" x 17" 4-page newspaper forms for students to fill in) would be helpful resources for completing this activity.

News Article

A reporter must make sure that all the important information is included in a news story. There are questions that will help you organize this information. They can be used as an outline or guide for taking notes and writing.

To prepare your students for writing their own news articles, use the following activities.

- Write the 5 W's (WHO, WHAT, WHEN, WHERE, WHY) and HOW on a chart or chalkboard.

- Provide the sentences which follow and ask students to identify the WHO, WHAT, WHERE, WHEN, WHY, or HOW from the bolded part of each sentence.

  _____ **Mrs. Smith, the school librarian,** helped them organize special activities for National Book Week.

  _____ They held a **Favorite Book Celebration.**

  _____ National Book Week is **November 13-17** this year.

  _____ The children in Room 8 decided to celebrate Book Week **because they enjoy reading so much.**

  _____ All the classes in Fernwood Elementary School participated in a Favorite Characters Parade **on the school playgrounds.**

  _____ The principal organized the classes **by grade level** for the parade.

- Supply students with some actual news stories from the newspaper. Have them read the stories and circle the answers to the WHO, WHAT, WHERE, WHEN, WHY, and HOW questions supplied in the story. Compare your students' findings.

  Then have the class work together to write a practice article by choosing a newsworthy story from *The Cricket in Times Square* (e.g. The fire in the newsstand, Chester Cricket's fame, Chester's disappearance at the end of the story). Discuss and write the answers to the 5 W's (and 1 H) next to the questions on the chalkboard.

- Explain that the information from these answers should appear in the first paragraph of a news story. This is where the reader will receive the most important information. The remaining paragraphs tend to contain less important information and usually support or further explain the first paragraph.

Have your students try these same techniques to complete their own news stories.

Feature Article

The feature section of your newspaper is where your students may show their creativity. A feature article can be an interview, a TV, movie, or book review, a cartoon, a fashion review, or most any other story of general interest which does not fall into another news category.

The 5 W's are not always emphasized in the beginning paragraph of a feature article. The goal is not to compact facts, but to make the story interesting and fun for the reader. The article should have a catchy and interesting introduction and a stimulating conclusion.

Have your class brainstorm some introductory paragraphs for an interview with Chester Cricket or a book review of *The Cricket in Times Square*. Write the introductory sentences on the board and vote on the catchiest phrase. Then have your students brainstorm some closing statements for the story. A suspenseful or surprising ending is sometimes a good way to peak a reader's interest.

Feature articles may be about people, travel, cooking, organizations, gardening, decorating, new products, etc. Features may require a lot of research and take a long time to prepare. To help students prepare for writing feature articles, have them choose one or more of the following activities.

> *List four important people who might have a feature written about them. Find out about one of them and write a paragraph.*

> *List four places you might like to travel. Choose one, research it, and write why a tourist would want to go there.*

> *List four foods you would like recipes for. Find and copy a recipe, including directions, for one of them.*

> *List four other feature articles that you might like to read in a newspaper. Research one of them and write a paragraph about it.*

After your students have practiced writing a news article and a feature, have them compare and contrast some articles from a real newspaper. Which stories are more fun to read? Which stories give you the important information quickest? Why do you think the articles are written in this manner?

Build a Newsstand!

A newsstand for paper distribution can be made from a refrigerator box. Stand the box on end, then cut a door in the side and a large window in the front of the box. The class can paint and decorate the box to look like a newsstand. The newsstand can be folded and moved to the cafeteria, hallway, playground, or other paper distribution location.

Students can take turns "selling" newspapers from the newsstand, as Mario did in *The Cricket in Times Square*. If your class produces its own school newspaper, the refrigerator box newsstand could become a central location for students to get their newspaper copies. Discuss what other items are sold at a newsstand. If you have a school store, perhaps arrangements can be made to sell some of the items from the school store at the newsstand.

Objective Test and Essay

Matching: Match these quotes with the characters who said them by writing the letter from the matching quotation on the line next the character.

1. _____ Mario
2. _____ Mama
3. _____ Chester
4. _____ Tucker
5. _____ Mr. Smedley

a. "Crickets are good luck—so I suppose ants are better luck. And cockroaches are the best luck of all. Throw it away."

b. "Why I believe I shall write a letter to the musical editor of the New York *Times*," he said. "They'd certainly be interested."

c. "If I ever retire from scrounging, it will be on a Friday."

d. "I guess I'm just feeling Septemberish. It's getting toward autumn now. And it's so pretty in Connecticut."

e. "I would like to buy a cricket cage if you have any."

True or False: Write true or false next to each statement below.

1. _____ Mario had always wanted a pet.

2. _____ Mama Bellini is not concerned with money.

3. _____ Tucker, Harry, Chester, and Mario all went to Chinatown to visit Sai Fong.

4. _____ Chester Cricket attracted people to the Bellinis' newsstand.

5. _____ Chester preferred to sleep in his matchbox rather than in his cage.

Short Answer: Write a short answer to the following questions.

1. Where did Mario find Chester?

_____

2. How much did Mario pay for the cricket cage?

_____

3. Who helped Chester replace the two dollar bill he ate in the Bellinis' newsstand?

_____

4. How did Chester learn new pieces of music for his concerts?

_____

5. Why did Chester decide to leave New York City?

_____

Essay: Write the answers to the following essay questions on the back of this page.

1. Choose the character from the story who you feel is the most dependable and responsible. Use examples from the story to support your choice.

2. Do you think the Bellini newsstand could have become successful without Chester's help? Why or why not?

Response

Identify the speaker and explain the meaning of the following quotes from *The Cricket in Times Square*.

Note to the teacher: Choose an appropriate number of quotes for your students to answer.

Chapter 2   " 'Please, Mama, I want to keep him for a pet.' "

Chapter 3   " 'They were having such a good time laughing and singing songs that they didn't notice me when I jumped into the picnic basket,...I was sure they wouldn't mind if I just had a taste.' "

Chapter 5   " 'That was a perfect middle C.' "

Chapter 6   " 'This velly ancient clicket cage. Once clicket who belonged to Empelor of all China lived in this cage.' "

Chapter 6   " 'You want Chinese Fortune cookie?' "

Chapter 7   " 'I'm sleeping on money inside the palace,' he said. 'It's a dream come true.' "

Chapter 8   " 'I dreamed it was a leaf and I ate it.' "

Chapter 8   " 'So for all the long years of my youth, when I could have been gamboling—which means playing with the other mousies, I saved. I saved paper, I saved food, I saved clothing—' "

Chapter 9   " 'Plenty leaves on tlee. I save all for clicket.' "

Chapter 10   " 'Any alarm in a fire.' "

Chapter 11   " 'He eats money—he commits arson! He's a jinx, that's what. He's good luck going backwards. And he's got to go.' "

Chapter 11   " 'Keep it up! Keep it up! .. .She's a sucker for sad songs.' "

Chapter 13   " 'Look at them all. There's a fortune in this. I wish one of us was big enough to pass the hat.' "

Chapter 14   " 'It's getting towards autumn now. And it's so pretty up in Connecticut. All the trees change color.' "

Chapter 15   " 'The bell's gone, ... You and I and the cricket were the only ones who knew where it was.' "

Cashing In *(Review)*

The following game is a fun way to review material before a traditional test, or to review the story at the end of the unit. Divide your class into 2 or 3 teams. Explain that each team will be given a turn to choose a category and money amount from the chart you have drawn on the chalkboard. The team will then be given 30 seconds to answer the category question they have chosen after it has been read. If the team is unable to respond or has an incorrect answer, the question remains on the board and can be chosen by another team. Have teams take turns choosing categories until all the questions have been answered. Keep score by adding the money amounts earned by each team. Team members, within the teams, should take turns choosing and answering questions. The questions that are worth more will tend to be more difficult.

Bellinis	Smorgas-bord	Chester	Money	Vocab.
$100	$100	$100	$100	$100
$200	$200	$200	$200	$200
$300	$300	$300	$300	$300
$400	$400	$400	$400	$400
$500	$500	$500	$500	$500

Draw this chart on your chalkboard. After a question has been answered, erase the money amount from the chart so it will not be chosen again.

The game questions are listed below. Answers are on page 48 in the answer key.

Bellinis

$100 What business do the Bellinis run?
$200 How does Mama Bellini feel about Chester the first time she sees him?
$300 Where is the Bellinis' newsstand located?
$400 How does Chester's playing help the Bellini family?
$500 What kind of music does Mama Bellini like?

Smorgasbord

$100 Why does Mario go to Chinatown?
$200 Why is Chester surprised by Tucker and Harry's friendship?
$300 How did Chester learn to play "human music"?
$400 What did Tucker use as a pillow the night he slept in the cricket cage?
$500 How did the fire in the newsstand start?

Chester

$100 How did Chester get from Connecticut to New York?
$200 How did Mario discover Chester?
$300 Why was Chester called a jinx?
$400 Describe one of the games Chester played with Mario.
$500 Explain how Chester makes his chirping sound.

Money

$100 How much did Mario pay for the cricket cage?
$200 How did Tucker manage to collect so much money?
$300 Why is money so important to Mama Bellini?
$400 Who helped Chester replace the two dollars he ate in the Bellinis' newsstand?
$500 Why do the Bellinis leave the cash register drawer in the newsstand open?

Vocabulary-Define the Word

$100 scrounging
$200 jinx
$300 eavesdropping
$400 amateur
$500 entomologist

Bibliography

Adair, Audrey J. *Musical Instruments & the Voices: Fifty Ready-to-Use Activities.* (Prentice Hall, 1987)

Anders, Rebecca. *Making Musical Instruments.* (Lerner Publications, 1975)

Beimer, Linda. *New York City: Our Community.* (Gibbs Smith Pub., 1986)

Cleary, Beverly. *Ralph S. Mouse.* (William Morrow & Company, 1982)

Cole, Joanna. *An Insect's Body.* (William Morrow & Company, 1984)

Earle, Olive. *Crickets.* (William Morrow & Company, 1956)

Englander, Roger. *Opera. What's all that Screaming About?* (Walker & Co., 1983)

Holder, Heidi. *Aesop's Fables.* (Viking Penguin, 1981)

Lawson, Robert. *Ben & Me.* (Dell, 1973

Rabbit Hill. (Penguin, 1977

Ling, Yu. *Cooking the Chinese Way.* (Lerner Publications, 1982)

Mar, S.Y. Lu. *Chinese Tales of Folklore.* (Criterion Books, 1964)

O'Brien, Robert. *Mrs. Frisby and the Rats of Nimh.* (Atheneum, 1971)

Patent, Dorothy Hinshaw. *How Insects Communicate.* (Holiday House, 1975)

Porter, Keith. *Discovering Crickets and Grasshoppers.* (Bookwright Press, 1986)

Posell, Elsa Z. *This is an Orchestra* (Houghton Mifflin, 1973)

Selden, George. *Chester Cricket's New Home.* (Dell Publishing, 1983)
Chester Cricket's Pigeon Ride. (Farrar, Straus and Giroux, 1981)
Harry Cat's Pet Puppy. (Farrar, 1974)
Harry Kitten and Tucker Mouse. (Farrar, Straus and Giroux, 1986)
The Meadow. (Farrar, Straus and Giroux, 1987)
Tucker's Countryside. (Dell Publishing, 1969)

Thompson, Amy Shui & Stuart. *Chinese Food & Drink.* (Bookwright Press, 1987)

Weng, M.A. Jagendorf and Virginia Weng. *The Magic Boat and Other Chinese Folk Stories.* (The Vanguard Press, 1980)

White, E.B. *Charlotte's Web.* (Harper & Row, 1952)
Stewart Little. (Harper & Row, 1945)
Trumpet of the Swan. (Harper & Row, 1970)

Answer Key

Page 10

1. Accept appropriate summaries.
2. Mario helps his family by working in his family's newsstand. He works especially late on Saturday nights.
3. (1) second hand radio - listening
   (2) box of facial tissues - Mama's hay fever
   (3) box of matches - lighting Papa's pipe
   (4) cash register - money
   (5) alarm clock - no good reason
4. Accept appropriate responses suggesting that Paul knows that Mario's family needs the money.
5. Accept appropriate characterizations including information about scrounging and eavesdropping.
6. Mario hears a sound like a violin coming from a corner near the stairs.
7. Mama is disgusted by Chester. She feels that he is a bug that carries diseases and should be thrown away.
8. He eats chocolate and liverwurst.
9. Accept appropriate explanations.
10. Accept reasonable summaries of Chester's trip in the picnic basket from Connecticut to New York.

Page 13

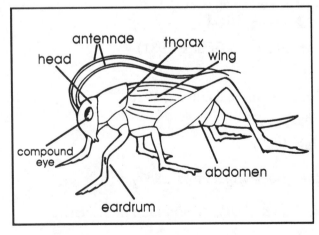

Page 15

1. Accept appropriate summaries.
2. In the country the cats and mice Chester knows are enemies.

3. The Bellinis' newsstand does not sell many newspapers or magazines, and the family makes very little money.
4. Chester is overwhelmed. He feels that the sights and sounds were too terrible and beautiful for a cricket used to the burble of a brook.
5. Chester ate leaves, grass, and sometimes tender bark.
6. Chester is a musician who played a perfect middle C with his wings.
7. Mario's friend, Jimmy Lebovski, told Mario that the Chinese like crickets.
8. Accept appropriate responses suggesting that Sai Fong likes crickets and is charmed by Mario's interest in crickets. Sai Fong knows that Mario is poor and he wants him to have the cricket cage.
9. Descriptive examples could include: old, Chinese, generous, wise, friendly, polite.
10. Accept appropriate explanations.

Page 20

1. Accept appropriate summaries.
2. He thinks the cage is beautiful and kingly. He is envious.
3. He finds Mama Bellini's earring in the cash register.
4. Accept appropriate answers: e.g., He's making new friends. Mario is taking care of him. He's enjoying learning about the city.
5. Steal and replace the money with bills from the lunch counter. Make it look like a thief had broken into the stand. Eat the rest and pretend nothing happened. Tape the edge to pass it as a one dollar bill.
6. Accept appropriate answers.
7. Sai Fong suggests that Chester eat mulberry leaves in order to "spin beautiful song."
8. They felt money was very important. They were stingy.

Answer Key *(cont.)*

Page 20 *(cont.)*

9. He is concerned about Chester's eating the $2.00 and he wants to ask Sai Fong about what a cricket should eat.

10. The food was traditional Chinese. He ate with chopsticks. He wore a robe. He drank tea. He bowed to greet his hosts.

Page 23

number of coins scrounged	15 coins	20 coins	44 coins	fewest possible coins	greatest number of possible coins
fifty cent pieces	3	0	2	5	0
quarters	4	8	4	1	0
dimes	3	9	3	1	0
nickels	2	0	7	1	0
pennies	3	3	28	3	293

The 44 coin column is more difficult and could be used as a challenge question.

Page 25

1. Accept appropriate summaries.

2. Liverwurst, slice of ham, 3 pieces of bacon, lettuce, tomato, bread, cole slaw, chocolate bar, iced soft drinks.

3. They have no refrigerator in which to make or store ice.

4. He listens to the radio in the newsstand.

5. Paul, the conductor.

6. She blames him for eating the two dollars and for starting the fire.

7. He invited Tucker and Harry to the newsstand and it was his music playing that made Tucker dance and knock over the matches.

8. Chester plays "Come Back to Sorrento," one of Mama's favorite songs. She couldn't

believe that anyone who played so beautifully could start a fire.

9. Mr. Smedley is surprised, amazed, and delighted.

10. Accept appropriate responses.

Page 30

1. Accept appropriate summaries.

2. People who read the article about Chester come to see him play and buy papers.

3. People would recognize familiar tunes and be more likely to stop and listen. It is more of an oddity if a cricket can learn and play "human" music.

4. He enjoys playing for the crowds, but he is nervous and upset by everyone looking at him.

5. He sees the date: September 1 and knows that autumn is coming. He sees a brown leaf flying in the wind. Someone tries to steal his bell.

6. Chester doesn't feel like playing.

7. People stop to listen. Traffic stops too.

8. Leap frog and hide and seek. (Descriptions of the games are in chapter 15).

9. He sees that the bell is gone.

10. Accept appropriate responses.

Page 31

To prepare samples you will need paper cups, tissues, rubber bands, and various ingredients (listed below). Place the ingredient into a cup and cover with a tissue. Use the rubber band to secure the tissue around the cup, as shown in the picture. Prepare 5 samples for each group in your class. Some ingredient suggestions are:

- lemon juice/slice
- cinnamon
- molasses
- peanut butter
- vinegar
- mustard
- banana
- garlic
- onion

Page 38

You may want to look into what computer programs are available at your school to help you edit, format, and print your newspaper.

Page 42

Matching

1. e   2. a   3. d
4. c   5. b

True or False

1. true
2. false-Mama Bellini is very concerned with money.
3. false-Only Chester and Mario went to Chinatown.
4. true
5. true

Short Answer

1. In a dirty corner of the subway station
2. 15 cents
3. Tucker (and Harry)
4. He listened to the radio.
5. He was homesick for the Connecticut countryside.

Essay

1. Accept all appropriate answers that are well explained and supported by examples from the story.
2. Accept fully explained responses.

Page 43 *(In order of chapter quotes)*

1. Mario	6. Tucker	11. Mama
2. Chester	7. Chester	12. Tucker
3. Mr. Smedley	8. Tucker	13. Tucker
4. Sai Fong	9. Sai Fong	14. Chester
5. Sai Fong	10. Chester	15. Mario

Accept all reasonable and well-supported answers.

Page 44

Bellinis

$100 Newsstand
$200 She thinks he is an ugly, dirty insect.
$300 Times Square subway station
$400 It attracts crowds and they buy newspapers.
$500 Opera—especially Italian

Smorgasbord

$100 To buy a cricket cage, or to find out what crickets eat
$200 Mice and cats are usually enemies.
$300 By listening to the radio
$400 Mama's earring
$500 Tucker was dancing and knocked over a box of matches.

Chester

$100 He jumped into someone's picnic basket and was carried on a train.
$200 He heard Chester chirping in the corner.
$300 Mama said he ate the two dollars and started the fire.
$400 Hide and seek or leap frog (Described in chapter 15)
$500 He rubs his wings together causing ridges to vibrate.

Money

$100 15 cents
$200 He scrounged coins that people had dropped.
$300 The newsstand was not attracting much business so the Bellinis' were not making much money.
$400 Tucker (and Harry)
$500 The drawer became stuck once and the family was unable to access the money. This was all the money the family had.

Vocabulary

$100   To gather by scavenging or foraging what others have left or lost
$200   One that brings bad luck
$300   To listen secretly to what others are saying
$400   One who lacks experience or competence; not a professional
$500   One who studies insects